KU-135-176

Contents

Which dog?

Dogs are popular pets and can bring a lifetime of happy memories. Most dogs are fun companions. All dogs need love, care and attention, but some breeds are more demanding than others.

Your home and lifestyle

Before you choose a family dog you need to think about how you live. Will the dog be alone during the day, or will someone be home to keep it company? Do you have a garden or do you live in a flat with no outside space? Some dogs get along well with other pets in the house. Others like to be the only pet. Dogs such as terriers are bred to chase small animals. They are more likely to run after cats!

Puppy or older dog

Puppies need a lot of attention. You will have to house-train a puppy and spend lots of time with it at first. You may find that an older dog is better suited to your family.

Rescue a dog!

Rescue centres are full of dogs and puppies that need new homes. Check your local centre to see if you can give a pet a forever home before you buy from a breeder.

The right dog for you?

☑ Will the dog have company during the day?

☑ Do you have the time to give an active dog lots of exercise every day?

☑ Can your family afford the food costs and vet bills?

☑ Do you have another pet in the home?

Read on ...

Dogs are great pets and they make loyal companions, but it is important to choose the right one for you. This book will help you to pick and care for your pet. Learn about four of popular breeds. Try your hand at making some tasty doggy treats. You will also find some fascinating facts about your new best friend!

What you will need

All dogs need some basic items. They need food and water bowls, a collar and lead and some toys. Your dog will also need a bed or crate to sleep in.

What you need

- ☑ Food and water bowls the right size for your dog.

- ☑ Collar with ID tag and a lead.

- ☑ Grooming brushes and comb.

- ☑ Pooper-scooper and poo bags. The law says you must pick up after your dog!

- ☑ Toys, such as tug-of-war rope, chew toys, balls and ball thrower.

- ☑ Bed or crate for sleeping.

Dog bowls

Food and water bowls should be large enough for your dog to get its mouth inside easily. Nonslip bases on bowls are useful, so your pooch does not push its food around the floor!

Metal bowls do not break.

Grooming

All dogs need grooming – some more than others. You will need a brush and comb especially for your dog. A slicker brush has small pins on it. They are good for getting tangles out of hair. An ordinary bristle brush is good for giving the coat shine.

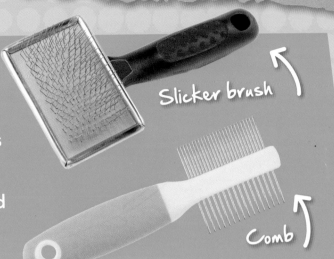

Slicker brush

Comb

Harnesses or collars?

If a dog pulls on the lead, the collar can put pressure on its neck and cause injury. A harness can be a better way to keep control of your dog on walks. A harness can help stop a dog pulling on the lead. Make sure you fit the right size harness for your dog.

Microchips

A microchip is placed under your dog's skin. The chip has a number that identifies your dog in case your pet gets lost. All dogs must have a microchip by the time they are 8 weeks old.

ID tag

Dogs in public spaces must wear an ID tag with the owner's surname and address on it. If your dog goes missing, an ID tag will help get your dog back to you quickly.

Feeding time

Your dog needs the right amount of food to keep it fit and healthy. It also needs a supply of clean water. How much to feed your pooch depends on its size, age and activity.

Titbits and treats

Rewarding good behaviour with a titbit or treat is a fun way for your dog to learn. You can buy treats specially for dogs in a pet shop. Most dogs also like small pieces of cheese and cooked chicken. Be careful not to overfeed your dog with treats!

All types of chews are tasty treats.

How much to feed

The feeding guide on your dog's food label tells you how much to feed your dog, depending on its weight. Make sure you measure your dog's food. Ask an adult to check your dog's weight every two to three weeks. If your dog is gaining or losing weight, you'll need to adjust the amount of food or exercise it has.

Wet or dry?

Some people like to feed their dogs tinned food. Other people prefer to give kibble (dried food). You can also feed your dog a mixture of both. Just be sure to give the right amounts for your dog's weight, age and daily activity. Puppies need to be fed about three or more times a day. Adult dogs should eat one or two meals a day.

Kibble (dried food)

Tinned meat meal

Complete dried food

Poison!

Some foods are poisonous for dogs. Never feed your dog grapes, onion, avocado, rhubarb, fruits with pits (such as peaches) or mushrooms. Chocolate can be poisonous, too. Cooking chocolate is more poisonous than milk chocolate or white chocolate.

Grooming and cleaning

Some dogs have thick, silky coats. Others have short, fluffy coats. Whatever breed your dog is, you need to groom it to remove dead hair. Almost all breeds moult twice every year. Some breeds do not moult, but they need to be groomed and clipped regularly.

Healthy teeth

Just like people, dogs need to have clean, healthy teeth. Ask an adult to help you clean your dog's teeth. You will need special toothpaste made for dogs – don't use ordinary toothpaste. You can use an old toothbrush or a finger brush. You may need to get your dog used to you handling its mouth at first. Pull up the dog's lips and brush the teeth gently. Work your way from front to back.

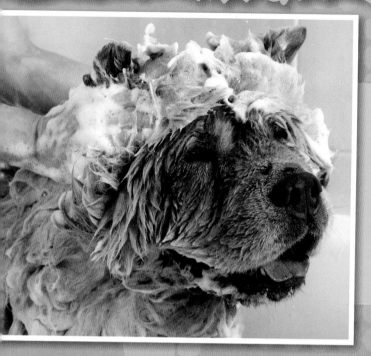

Bathtime

If you need to give your dog a bath, use a mild baby shampoo or a special shampoo for dogs. Make sure you rinse all the shampoo out with warm water. Have a dog towel ready for the big shake-off!

Getting rid of tangles

Use a comb or slicker brush to detangle your dog's coat. Comb out any dead hair from the undercoat. Then brush the coat, starting at the head and working towards the back. Gently brush your dog's chest and tummy area. Brush down the legs to the feet.

Ticks and fleas

Ask an adult to help check and remove any ticks. Ticks carry diseases. If you see flea dirt – small, dark specks on the skin – ask an adult to give your dog some antiflea treatment.

Exercise

All dogs need exercise to stay healthy and in shape. Some breeds, such as the Border Collie, need lots of exercise. Others, such as the Lhasa Apso, are happier on the sofa. Two to three walks a day will keep most dogs in shape.

Playtime

Lots of dogs love to play. Different breeds like different types of games and activities. Retrievers enjoy playing fetch games with a ball or favourite toy. Greyhounds like to chase things. Terriers were bred to find rats or foxes, so they often like sniffing and digging about.

Puppies

Your puppy cannot be taken for a walk until it has had all its jabs. Until then, you can carry it about in your arms to introduce it to noises and smells in the outside world.

Older dogs

As dogs age, they still need regular exercise. They might not walk as far as they used to, but they will enjoy going out. Walking will help prevent them putting on weight and keep their joints mobile.

Off lead

Dogs love being free to explore off the lead. They will travel three to four times further than you do. Train your dog to come back when called. Only let your dog off the lead in a safe place away from traffic. Some parks do not allow dogs to be off the lead.

Training

A well-trained dog is a pleasure to know. A badly behaved one can be a nuisance, even dangerous. Reward your dog when it gets things right. If training is fun, your dog will be more likely to learn what you want it to do.

Good practice

Use a happy voice to tell your dog what you want it to do. Use the same words each time. Reward the behaviour you want as soon as it happens. First reward small steps, such as moving in the right direction. Then reward the whole action, such as coming when called.

Rewards

You can use treats, toys, praise or play as rewards for good behaviour.

House-training a puppy

Learn the signs that your puppy wants to go to the toilet, such as walking in circles. Let the puppy outside and praise it when it goes to the toilet in the right place. Put down a sheet of newspaper if you live in a flat. When the puppy has learned to use it, put the paper outside. Praise the puppy when it relieves itself outside.

Basic commands

There are some basic commands all dogs should learn. These are coming when called, sit, lie down, walking on a loose lead, leave and stay. When your dog has learned the basics, you can train it to do fun tricks such as shaking a paw.

Short sessions

Keep your training sessions short. Practise for a few minutes each time, several times a day. Before long, you will have the best-trained dog in the area!

Staying healthy

You can help your dog stay healthy by making sure it gets enough exercise and its jabs are up to date. Even so, dogs get sick sometimes. just like people.

Fleas and worms

Make sure your pet is up to date with antiflea and worming treatments. Fleas can cause severe itching and allergies in your dog. Fleas can also pass on tapeworms. These parasites can cause illness if left untreated.

Coat and skin

When you groom your dog, look out for rough or red patches of skin. Also check for bald or thinning patches on your dog's coat. If your dog starts to scratch itself more than usual, or chews its paws, take it to the vet. In most cases, the vet can treat your dog's skin and coat problems with medicine.

A visit to the vet

Take your dog to the vet once a year for its booster shots and a check-up. The vet will ask questions about your dog's general health and any problems it may have. Take along some treats so your dog has good memories of its visit to the vet.

Paw problems

Check your dog's paws regularly for any problems. Look for cuts, scratches, thorns or grass seeds. If your dog is constantly licking its paws, it may have an injury.

Jabs

Puppies are usually vaccinated against disease when they are six to eight weeks old. They will need follow-up jabs, and then booster jabs every year to prevent disease.

In the wild

People have bred dogs for thousands of years. Today, there are hundreds of different breeds. Although there is such a huge variety, all pet dogs are descended from wolves.

Wolf pack

Wolves live in packs of at least two animals, usually more. Each wolf knows its place, or rank. The strong, or dominant, wolves are called alpha dogs. They get first choice on everything, including eating first and choosing where to sleep. Lower-ranking dogs treat them with respect.

Dingoes

Dingoes are semi-wild dogs that live in Australia. They live alone or in packs of up to 10 dogs. As with wolves, there are alpha dogs and pack rules.

The family pack

For your dog, your family is the pack. Your pet will pick up signals about who is in charge. It should be the lowest member of the pack. If a dog thinks it ranks high, there can be problems such as growling, snarling or biting.

The friendly wolf

Most dog breeds do not look like wolves. Yet dogs' behaviour and the way they communicate with each other are based on how wolves live. Think of your pet as a friendly wolf, and you'll understand each other just fine.

Pack rules

☑ Don't feed your dog titbits from the table.

☑ Don't let it sit on furniture or sleep on your bed unless it is invited.

☑ Feed your dog at feeding time, not when it demands to be fed.

☑ Teach your dog to wait while you go first through doorways.

☑ Use clear instructions and reward your dog when it obeys them.

Labrador Retriever

The Labrador retriever, or Lab, is the most popular breed in the United Kingdom. It is friendly, affectionate and intelligent. Labs make an ideal family pet. They also make excellent guide dogs for blind and partially sighted people.

The Lab loves children.

Where in the world?

This loyal and reliable pooch comes from Newfoundland in Canada. The local fishermen used Labs to pull in their nets loaded with fish. Labs love water and go swimming any time they get the chance. They have a water-resistant coat, which keeps them warm.

Breed profile

Labradors are strongly built. They are about 56 cm tall at the shoulder. The coat is short, straight and thick. It comes in solid colours of black, yellow or chocolate. Labs usually live to age 10 to 12 years.

Looking after me

Labs are patient, reliable and gentle. They are best suited to living in a family house with a garden.

- ☑ Labs enjoy family life, are gentle with children and are easily trained.

- ☑ Labs need plenty of space and exercise. They are not suited to living in a small flat.

Miniature Schnauzer

Active, lively and friendly, the Miniature Schnauzer is the smallest of the schnauzer breeds. 'Schnauze' is German for 'muzzle'. Farmers used these dogs to catch rats. Schnauzers are also very keen guard dogs.

The Miniature Schnauzer is friendly and clever.

Where in the world?

The Miniature Schnauzer comes from Germany and was first bred in the mid- to late 1800s. It is a mix between the bigger standard schnauzer and smaller breeds such as the Affenpinscher.

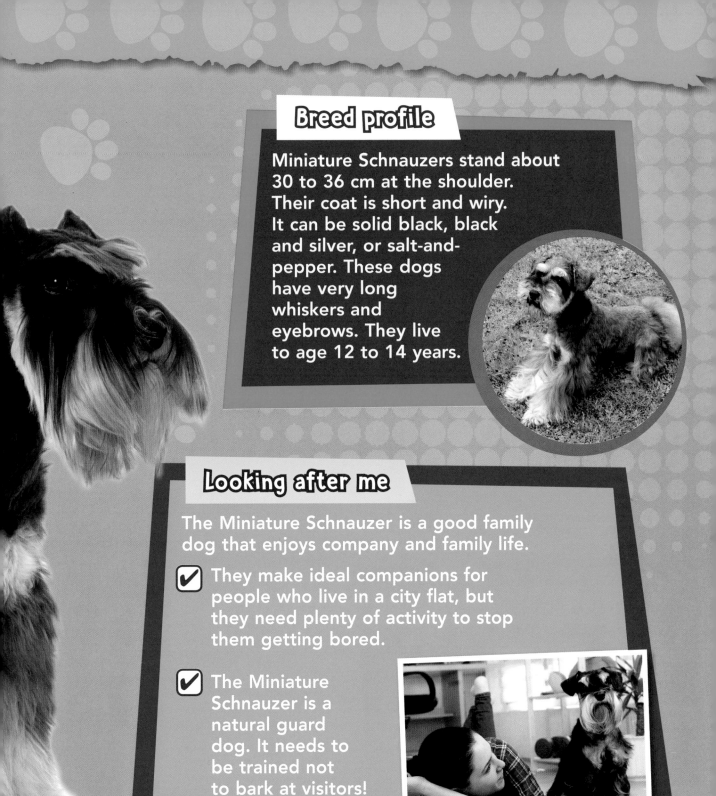

Breed profile

Miniature Schnauzers stand about 30 to 36 cm at the shoulder. Their coat is short and wiry. It can be solid black, black and silver, or salt-and-pepper. These dogs have very long whiskers and eyebrows. They live to age 12 to 14 years.

Looking after me

The Miniature Schnauzer is a good family dog that enjoys company and family life.

- ☑ They make ideal companions for people who live in a city flat, but they need plenty of activity to stop them getting bored.

- ☑ The Miniature Schnauzer is a natural guard dog. It needs to be trained not to bark at visitors!

Shetland Sheepdog

Popularly known as the Sheltie, the Shetland Sheepdog was originally bred for herding sheep. Alert and intelligent, it is a popular family pet all over the world.

The Sheltie responds well to obedience training.

Where in the world?

The Shetland Sheepdog comes from the Shetland Islands, off the northern coast of Scotland. The thick coat of the Sheltie is well suited to the cold winter climate of these islands. The islands are also home to a miniature breed of pony.

Breed profile

The Sheltie stands about 36 cm at the shoulder. It has thick white hair around the neck. The coat comes in different colours, including tan and white and black and white. Shelties live to age 11 to 13 years.

Looking after me

Shelties are full of energy and need lots of exercise.

- ☑ They are often shy with strangers at first.

- ☑ Shelties are gentle with children and affectionate.

Jack Russell Terrier

A small, lively dog that loves long walks, the Jack Russell has bags of energy. It is affectionate but not suitable for families with other pets or young children.

Where in the world?

The Jack Russell was first bred in England in the 1800s by the Reverend (Parson) Jack Russell. He liked fox hunting. The dog was trained to go down foxholes to chase out foxes. The dog had to run fast enough to keep up with the hunting horses.

Breed profile

Jack Russells stand 25 to 36 cm at the shoulder. They have thick smooth or wirehaired coats. The thick coat keeps the dog warm in cold weather. Jack Russells are usually white with black, lemon or tan markings. They live to age 12 to 15 years.

The Jack Russell is intelligent and loyal but can be 'snappy'.

Looking after me

Very active and outgoing, Jack Russells need lots of exercise and training.

☑ They need to be occupied and should not be left alone for long periods. If they get bored, they will start chewing anything they can find.

☑ They can be noisy guard dogs, so will need to be trained to stop barking at your visitors!

Make it !
Doggy treats

You can make these delicious biscuit treats for your dog. Ask an adult to help when it's time to take the biscuits out the oven. Your pooch will love them!

You will need:

360 g wholewheat flour

1 teaspoon garlic salt

120 ml soft bacon fat

120 g grated cheese

1 egg, beaten slightly

240 ml milk

1 Ask an adult to help preheat the oven to 200°C (400°F/gas mark 6).

2 Put the flour and garlic salt in a large mixing bowl.

3 Stir in the bacon fat. Then add the cheese and egg.

4 Gradually add enough milk to form a dough.

5 Knead the dough and roll it out to about 25 mm thick.

6 Use a cookie cutter to cut out the dough or cut out shapes with a butter knife.

7 Place the dough pieces on a greased cookie sheet. Bake in a preheated oven for about 12 minutes, until they start to brown.

When they are cool, offer a biscuit to your dog as a yummy treat!

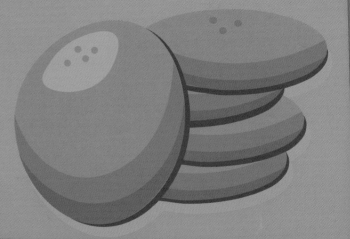

Did you know?

The UK Kennel Club currently recognizes 218 dog breeds. The Fédération Cynologique Internationale (FCI) is the biggest dog organization in the world. It recognizes 332 breeds. That is the number of breeds that most kennel clubs worldwide recognize.

Dogs can hear sounds that are about four times further away than humans can hear.

Dogs only have sweat glands in their paws. They have to pant to cool down on hot days. It can help to wet the pads of your dog's paws when it's hot.

The average dog can learn 165 words. A Border Collie named Chaser learned the names of 1,022 items – more than any other animal.

Some popular new crossbreeds include Labradoodles, Yorkipoos, Cavapoos, Cockapoos and Schnoodles.

Dogs are the most popular pets in the United Kingdom. About 25 percent of households own a dog. That's about 8.5 million pooches!

A dog's sense of smell is 10,000 to 100,000 times better than a human's. Some dogs have been trained to sniff out diseases such as cancer and diabetes in people.

Dogs have 42 teeth. That's 10 more than an adult human and 22 more than a child.

Glossary

breed (1) to take care of a group of animals to produce more animals of a particular kind. (2) a particular kind of animal that has been produced by breeding.

breeder person who breeds certain animals, such as dogs.

flea very small biting insect that lives on animals.

ID tag short for 'identification' tag, and worn on the pet's collar.

house-train to train an animal to go to the toilet outside or in the correct place.

jabs *see* **vaccination**

moult to lose hair and replace it with new growth.

parasite an animal that lives in or on another animal and gets food from it.

pooper-scooper device for picking up dog poop.

rank position in a group.

slicker brush brush with fine wire pins used for untangling hair.

smell receptor area in the nose that detects smells.

sweat gland area of the body that produces sweat.

tapeworm long, flat worm that lives in the stomachs of animals and people.

tick very small insect that attaches itself to a larger animal and feeds on it.

toxic poisonous or harmful.

undercoat a layer of short hair growing underneath the longer outer coat.

vaccination treatment with a substance, called a vaccine, to protect against a particular disease.

Further resources

Books

Caring for Dogs and Puppies,
Ben Hubbard (Watts, 2015)

Dogs (Animal Abilities), Charlotte Guillain
(Raintree, 2014)

Looking After Dogs and Puppies (Pet Guides),
Katherine Starke (Usborne, 2013)

Websites

www.bbc.co.uk/cbbc/thingstodo/pet-school-facts-dog
This BBC website has information and fun facts about dogs.

www.bluecross.org.uk/advice/dog
Lots of information and advice from the Blue Cross on how
to train your dog and keep it healthy.

www.thekennelclub.org.uk
The Kennel Club has lots of information about dogs,
including profiles of different breeds.

Index